P9-BJG-616

DATE DUE

ASE	JAN 25		
ASE	FEB 04		
NO MORE REN			
EAG	MAR 27		
MNJG	APR 27		
SL8	APR 30		
VnS	OCT 21		
mG	JAN 09		
TNJ	FEB 13		
AJ8			
RCN	MAR 08		
S5	MAR 10		
GR	APR 02		
NPY			

DEMCO 38-296

Yellow Umbrella Books are published by Capstone Press
151 Good Counsel Drive, P.O. Box 669, Mankato, Minnesota 56002
http://www.capstone-press.com

Library of Congress Cataloging-in-Publication Data
Trumbauer, Lisa, 1963–
    At school/by Lisa Trumbauer; consulting editor, Gail Saunders-Smith.
    p. cm.
    Includes index.
    ISBN 0-7368-0741-1
    1. Education (Elementary)—United States—Juvenile literature. 2. School children—
United States—Juvenile literature. [1. Schools.] I. Saunders-Smith, Gail. II. Title.
LB1556.T78   2001
372.973—dc21   00-036676

Summary: Describes how kids travel to school, what they do in the classroom, and
subjects they study.

Editorial Credits:
Susan Evento, Managing Editor/Product Development; Elizabeth Jaffe, Senior Editor;
    Sydney Wright and Charles Hunt, Designers; Kimberly Danger and Heidi Schoof,
    Photo Researchers

Photo Credits:
Cover: Llewellyn/Pictor; Title Page: Visuals Unlimited/Steve Strickland; Page 2: Index Stock
Imagery (top), Pictor (bottom); Page 3: Unicorn Stock Photos/Tom & Dee Ann McCarthy;
Page 4: International Stock; Page 5: Pictor (top & bottom); Page 6: Shaffer Photography/James
L. Shaffer; Page 7: Visuals Unlimited/Jeff Greenberg (left), Ron Chapple/FPG International
LLC (right); Page 8: International Stock/Vessey/Vanderberg; Page 9: Photo Network/Tom
McCarthy; Page 10: Visuals Unlimited/R. Perron (top), Morris Best/Pictor (bottom); Page 11:
Photo Network/Tom McCarthy; Page 12: Charles Gupton/Pictor (top), Pictor (bottom); Page
13: Shaffer Photography/James L. Shaffer (left), Bob Daemmrich/Pictor (right); Page 14: Kent
& Donna Dannen; Page 15: Visuals Unlimited/Jeff Greenberg (left), FPG International LLC
(right); Page 16: International Stock/Scott Barrow

1 2 3 4 5 6 06 05 04 03 02 01

At School

By Lisa Trumbauer

Consulting Editor: Gail Saunders-Smith, Ph.D.
Consultants: Claudine Jellison and Patricia Williams,
Reading Recovery Teachers
Content Consultant: Andrew Gyory, Ph.D., American History

Yellow Umbrella Books

an imprint of Capstone Press
Mankato, Minnesota

Some kids walk to school.

Some kids take the bus
to school.

How do you get to school?

It is fun to come
into the classroom
to be with our friends.

It is time for the morning
meeting. We find out
what we will do today.

We learn from our teachers and from each other.

We begin by meeting
in small groups.
The teacher works
with each group
to teach reading.

The rest of us work
at learning centers.
This helps us learn by
ourselves and with classmates.

This group
learns about
plants.

He learns
how letters
make words.

The teacher asks us to look at the clock to read the time. It is time to go to art class.

Other days we go to music class.

Now it is time for lunch.
We are hungry.

We have recess after lunch.

We hear the bell.
It is time to line up and go
inside to do math games.
We are learning
how to add numbers.

Then we go to the library.
The librarian reads us a story.

We look at the globe
to see where the story
takes place.

Next, we have gym class.
We exercise and learn
how to play games.

Some days our class learns
outside of school.
We go on field trips.
Today we learn
about the birds in our park.

Before we know it,
the school day ends.
Some kids go to after-school
activities to learn sports
or about computers.

Then we all go home
to get ready for
another day of school.

What do you like to learn
at school?

Words to Know/Index

classmate—a person who is in the same class as another person; page 7

classroom—a place in a school where teachers and students meet; page 3

computer—an electronic machine that can store information; page 15

exercise—activity that helps keep people fit and healthy; page 13

field trip—a group outing to learn about something firsthand; page 14

globe—a round model of Earth; page 12

gym—a class in which students exercise and learn sports; page 13

hungry—wanting food; page 10

learning center—an area in a classroom where students explore a subject or practice a skill; page 7

library—a place where books, newspapers, encyclopedias, and other materials are kept for reading or borrowing; page 12

recess—a break from school or work to play or to rest; page 10

Word Count: 263
Early-Intervention Levels: 9-12